Is Human Life Special?

Gary Bates
and
Lita Cosner

ABOUT THE AUTHORS:

Gary Bates is the CEO of *Creation Ministries International (US)*. He has been speaking on the creation/evolution topic since 1990 and has authored dozens of articles for CMI's popular website, creation.com. His book, *Alien Intrusion: UFOs and the Evolution Connection,* is the only creationist book to have been a top 50 Amazon.com bestseller. He also co-authored three other creation books, including the children's book *One Big Family* with his wife Frances. They have four adult children.

Lita Cosner earned an M.A. (New Testament) from Trinity Evangelical Divinity School and is the Information Officer and New Testament specialist for *Creation Ministries International (US)*. Her passion is explaining the Bible in a way that is understandable to the average Christian, as well as showing the unity of Scripture demonstrated by the New Testament authors' use of the Old Testament.

Other booklets by Gary and Lita:
How did we get the Bible? And is it the Word of God?
Gay Marriage: Right or Wrong? And who decides?

Is Human Life Special?

First printing: 2015
© 2015 by *Creation Ministries International (US)*

Published by:
Creation Book Publishers
P.O. Box 350
Powder Springs, GA, 30127, USA.
Phone: 1-800-616-1264
creationbookpublishers.com

TABLE OF CONTENTS

Many people are concerned at the obvious trend today of devaluing life. Abortion has been legalized for decades, resulting in the death of millions of innocent unborn children every year, and now, arguments for euthanasia and assisted suicide are gaining sympathy in the media. How did this happen, when Western[1] culture would have found these sorts of things horrifying just 100 years ago?

Evolution devalues human life

It might be surprising to hear that this is the logical outcome of the belief that humans have evolved; if we have evolved from animals, how are we worth more than them? Not everyone immediately considers whether they are the product of evolutionary processes over millions of years. But, everyone has asked the fundamental 'big question' of 'How did it all begin?' at some time. Such ideas are often framed as 'The three big questions of life':

1. Where did I come from?
2. What is the meaning of life / my purpose?
3. What happens when we die?

If you think about the 'three big questions', you will realize that the answers to questions two and three will be determined by what you believe about question one. If life evolved, there is no purpose to it except that which you make up. And, if this material universe is all that there is, there is nothing to look forward to after death. You are born, you live, you die, and that's it, but if you are lucky, perhaps you will get recycled as packaged fish food! However, if God created humans, then He defines the purpose of life, and He determines what happens to us when we die.

The historical basis for valuing life

Historically, Western society was founded upon Christian morality, which implied accountability to the Creator God of the Bible. And one foundational idea was that mankind was created in the image of God their Creator. This is obvious because only humans have the capacity to think about the 'three big questions' and to have a relationship with our Creator. Endowed with this image, it therefore follows that people have value and rights that animals do not have.

Genesis 1–2 also teaches that God declared mankind, His final creation on Day 6, to be the stewards of His creation. This means that we can use creation for our benefit, but we also have to take care of it, because it belongs to God who put us in charge of it. Put another way, we are 'top dog' because it was planned that way, and it is not by cosmic chance.

By contrast, evolutionists view mankind as merely another evolved animal. Under this view, the only reason that humans are at the top of the evolutionary tree is because we evolved to be better adapted and fitter than our competitors. This is a naturalistic and atheistic view of our origins, and although some earlier evolutionary views were around long before Darwin, he certainly popularized this naturalistic view of our world. The elevation of Darwinism has had tragic consequences for human beings.

But isn't evolution 'science'?

The debate about origins still rages 150 plus years after Charles Darwin published *On the Origin of Species* in 1859. Until Darwin, most people in Western nations, including the great founding fathers of our modern scientific disciplines like Newton, Faraday, Pasteur, and Kepler, believed that the universe and all life on earth were created by the Creator God of the Bible.

Today, most people have accepted Darwinian evolution as fact, believing it is a modern, scientific approach for interpreting our world.

But for many it is simply because evolution is all they have ever been taught. Under the banner of 'modern science', concepts of creation are excluded from public education because they are mistakenly regarded as unscientific. While it is beyond the scope of this little booklet to discuss the mountains of information pertaining to the creation/ evolution debate, it is worth just diverting a little to define what science actually is. Can the scientific method actually tell us what happened at the beginning of it all? This is foundational when considering whether human life is more valuable than animal life.

In the 18th century, many discoveries about our world were being made, and a movement called the 'Enlightenment' grew out of Western Europe. Many philosophers and thinkers sought to explain their world without reference to a higher authority or deity. Instead, they appealed to nature itself (philosophical naturalism), materialism, or the idea that matter is all there ever was or will be. They paved the way for a more 'rational' approach of disbelief in a Creator God. Darwin's family was greatly influenced by these thinkers, and it would be fair to say that he was a product of his time. Soon, materialistic dogmatism invaded the scientific realm, and to this day it retains a firm grasp on every aspect of the sciences. World-renowned former Oxford Professor, author, and atheist Richard Dawkins wrote:

> "Darwin made it possible to be an intellectually fulfilled atheist."[2]

But, is this correct? Did Darwin discover the 'evolutionary' truth about life—that the universe and life can be explained without reference to God—using the scientific method?

What is science?

Evolution is not really 'science' as most commonly understand the term; to understand why, we have to think about what science actually is. When most people hear the word 'science', they often think of some of the marvelous scientific advances that have been made. We can launch satellites into orbit that allow us to beam television programs into our living rooms from other parts of the world. Or we can develop modern medicines and develop incredible technologies to help heal the sick. These advancements required observation, extrapolation, experimentation, and time. For example, if we were to test the boiling point of water, we would discover it boils at 100° C (212° F) at sea level. When the water boils, we can see steam escaping. We could hypothesize that if we captured the steam, we might be able to use it to turn a turbine wheel and generate power. Technologies are the result of continuing to test and build upon former ideas. We would call this *operational* or *experimental science.*

This is vastly different than trying to work out what happened in the past, and the longer we are disconnected from the past, the more difficult this becomes. For example, it is said that lifeless chemicals somehow self-organized to form the first primordial cell, and this was the ancestor of all life on earth. This is a hypothesis, but despite the countless man-hours and money spent to try and prove this idea, no experiment has shown this can happen via unguided natural processes (or indeed even with intelligence guiding the process!). In short, if one cannot observe it happening or test it and repeat it, then it falls outside of the commonly understood definition of science. Such ideas about evolution, that fish evolved into reptiles that became mammals that became apes that became humans, cannot be observed, tested, or repeated. As such, they fall under the category of beliefs about the past. This is important, because both evolutionists and creationists use such beliefs when interpreting their world and mankind's place in it, and, indeed, whether human life is special or not. One might call this *origins* or *historical science.*

OPERATIONAL/ EXPERIMENTAL SCIENCE	EVOLUTION OR CREATION
Happens in the present	Happened in the past
Can be observed	Was not observed
Can be repeated	Happened one time
Can be tested	Cannot be tested

Although many skeptical atheists claim there is no distinction in common practice, this is not true. Famous Harvard evolutionary biologist, Dr E.O. Wilson, wrote:

"If a moving automobile were an organism, functional biology would explain how it is constructed and operates, while evolutionary biology would reconstruct its origin and history—how it came to be made and its journey thus far."[3]

But, there are more foundational problems with trying to use science to figure out things that happened in the past. "Where did we come from?" is a *historical* question, so *historical* methods, not scientific ones, are needed, though science will obviously have some things to say about the subject.

Can we use science to determine the truth about where we came from?

Evolution is the dominant origins story in our culture. But Darwin did not have access to the marvelous technological insights we have today due to the advances of operational science. For example, Darwin had little idea about the complexity of the cell when compiling his ideas of evolution. We now know that the study of living cells is more like information technology, but only mind-blowingly more complex. In the nucleus of every living cell is the DNA molecule, which is basically a storage system that contains coded operational instructions for the almost countless functions in the cell. In a human cell, there are about 3 billion 'letters' of information, all ordered and arranged. It's analogous to a 1,000-volume instruction manual.

The words you are reading are composed of letters. But the letters by themselves do not contain information. They have to be arranged and ordered into words and sentences to produce meaningful information that you are reading and can understand. Random letters on this page would not convey meaningful information to you. As one hallmark that life was created, let's just take the DNA molecule. It is a storage system that contains multiple layers of sophisticated computer codes to help build cells. It will define whether to build a frog or a fish, a hippopotamus or a human being. We also now know that DNA has coded instructions for the building of 'machines' in the cell. Many of these machines actually help to repair the DNA that contains the instructions to build them in the first place! This is an inescapable 'chicken-and-egg' problem. So, in one sense, even though all life is 'just chemistry', it is the unfathomable, complex *arrangement* of chemical molecules that gives life. When one sees such layers of complex information (like the words in this booklet), one also instinctively knows that it came from an intelligent information-giver. If human anatomy and genetics display the scientific hallmarks of being designed, it ultimately means we were created. And Scripture tells us we were created for a reason. Thus, human life must be special in the eyes of our Creator.

DNA structure

Who decides who should live or die?

If you were to ask someone 'Is murder wrong?', most people would agree that it is, whether they are atheist or Christian. But if challenged, could the atheist provide a logical and consistent reason for why he or she thinks it is always objectively wrong? Today, in many countries, doctors are allowed to provide seriously ill people (or sometimes just hugely depressed people) medication that allows them to take their own lives. In some cases, the doctors or nurses will actually administer the lethal 'medication'.

The Hippocratic Oath is one of the most widely known Greek medical documents, and its principles still influence modern medical care. At its core is the principle of the caring for and saving of human life. One of the lines of the oath states, "Nor shall any man's entreaty prevail upon me to administer poison to anyone; neither will I counsel any man to do so." This is because there has always been a very clear distinction between medicine, which has the goal of healing and extending life where possible, and the destruction of life by poison and abortion (which the Hippocratic Oath also condemns).

Hippocrates

It is clear that there has been a 'shifting of the goalposts' to justify the lawful killing of individuals on certain occasions. Many euthanasia advocates claim that a person's quality of life is the deciding factor as to whether a life should continue or not. Increasingly, if someone wants to die because of illness, aging, or even depression, it is argued that allowing them to commit suicide with medical assistance is simply respecting their autonomy. But this is a very dangerous and artificial area to venture into, because who decides? Societies that offer voluntary euthanasia might quickly end up applying it to people who cannot request or consent to euthanasia, like small children and seniors suffering from Alzheimer's. And when euthanasia becomes acceptable in a society, very quickly someone's 'right to die' can become 'their duty to die', particularly if their care might be deemed an economic burden for society. For instance, the Nazi regime of Adolf Hitler considered mentally handicapped or disabled people to be inferior and a burden on society. At the heart of Nazi ideology was Darwinism's misguided concepts of 'survival of the fittest'. Indeed, in *Mein Kampf* (My Struggle), Hitler wrote:

> "Man must realize that a fundamental law of necessity reigns throughout the whole realm of Nature and that his existence is subject to the law of eternal struggle and strife. He will then feel that there cannot be a separate law for mankind in a world in … where the strong are always the masters of the weak and where those subject to such laws must obey them or be destroyed … He who wants to live must fight and who does not want to fight in this world where eternal struggle is the law of life has no right to exist."[4]

By making humans subject to this evolutionary view, Hitler's regime systematically killed tens of thousands of disabled people because their survival was deemed not to be in the best interests of the nation and his ideology of breeding a 'master' or superior race. In the same way, he regarded Jewish people, gypsies, and black people as inferior. Propaganda films of the day[5] showed images of handicapped people with the statement:

> "All weak living things will inevitably perish in nature. In the last few decades, mankind has sinned frightfully against the law of natural selection. We haven't just maintained life unworthy of life, we have even allowed it to multiply!"[6]

Both Jews and handicapped people were rounded up, shot, or sent to the gas chambers to be executed because the Nazis did not want their 'inferior genes' to multiply. We look back with abject horror at what happened and think that this could never happen again. Indeed, it is hard to believe that seemingly normal German soldiers who worked in concentration camps, who probably had their own wives and families, could shoot women (some of them pregnant) or children and babies and then roll their bodies into mass graves. What could switch a person's inbuilt conscience 'off' in such a way?

A faulty belief about where we came from can do this. Based upon a foundation of evolution, they were taught that their victims were sub-human, so they were not really killing people. When the leading Nazi chiefs were put on trial after the war, many protested their innocence by claiming

Mass grave at Bergen-Belsen Nazi concentration camp

that they had done nothing wrong and were just following the laws of their land as established by their government. And it would be naïve to think that the laws cannot be changed again to allow killing of 'less valuable' people.

In fact, this is already happening. The Netherlands allows euthanasia of infant children who, in the opinion of two doctors and the parents, are suffering unbearably and have no prognosis for improvement.[7] Belgium allows minors who are able to understand what is happening to them to request euthanasia.[8] And while most euthanasia legislation has strict requirements for who qualifies for euthanasia, in practice, these controls are not consistently followed. For instance, in Belgium "many euthanasia killings are imposed without request or consent".[9]

Evolutionary genocide

Interestingly, although many critics like to point to religious wars as the cause of much grief in the world, history shows that the 20th century was the most blood-stained in all of recorded history. And 150 million died because of anti-Christian, genocidal autocrats who built their political systems based upon the prevailing 'scientific' views of the day; that is, evolutionism and the idea that the strong should prevail. See box. As another author commented on this topic:

> "The greatest evil does not result from people zealous for God. It results when people are convinced there is no God to whom they must answer."[10]

A timeline of evolution-inspired terror[11]
Note: The death tolls cited below exclude direct war casualties.

1860: Karl Marx

The 'spiritual father' of communism, Marx was an avid Darwinist who combined his social and economic ideas with evolutionary principles. Marx wrote that *Origin of Species* "contains the basis in natural history for our views."[12] His disciple Lenin applied utter ruthlessness and terror in Russia—the term 'rivers of blood' has commonly been applied in describing his reign, and it has been estimated that the communist regime that Marx inspired led to the murder of over 100 million people.[13]

1918: Leon Trotsky

Fanatically committed to Darwinism and Marxism, communist leader Trotsky was brutal against religion of all forms, including the Christian church, leading the Red Army's torture squad. He said that Darwin's ideas "intoxicated" him, and "Darwin stood for me like a mighty doorkeeper at the entrance to the temple of the universe."[14] With no Creator's laws to restrain him and the justification of evolution, he felt free to use any means to attain power and political ends.

1930: Joseph Stalin

The world's worst mass-murderer studied at Tiflis (Tbilisi) Georgia, a theological college, but became an atheist after reading Darwin. After understanding that evolution provided no basis for conscience or morals, and following Lenin, he felt free to torture and murder to whatever extent he chose to achieve his communist goals. Deaths attributed to atheistic, communist ideology vary greatly simply because in most cases no records were kept and dissenters were conveniently disposed of. Between 1917 and 1959, under Lenin, Stalin, and Krushchev, the estimates vary from a low of 28 million to as high as almost 127 million.[15] Under Stalin alone, it is claimed that over 42 million were murdered.[16]

1940: Adolf Hitler

He formed his racial and social policies on the evolutionary ideas of survival of the fittest and the superiority of certain 'favoured races'. Hitler's reign resulted in the murder of 6 million Jews as well as many blacks, gypsies, the mentally impaired, and other groups deemed unfit to live—commonly known as the Holocaust. The evolutionary 'science' of eugenics provided him with justification for his decrees.

1949: Mao Zedong

Mao converted to Marxism/Leninism while working at Peking University and founded the People's Republic of China in 1949. During his 'Great Leap Forward', his anti-imperialist ideas led to wholesale reclamation of land from its owners and the removal of wealth from those he regarded as 'counter-revolutionaries'. This led to the greatest famine in Chinese history along with mass executions of those he believed were opposed to his ideas. In showing his allegiance to Marxist ideology, Mao wrote to his followers: "You'd better have less conscience. Some of our comrades have too much mercy, not enough brutality, which means that they are not so Marxist. On this matter, we indeed have no conscience! Marxism is that brutal … We are prepared to sacrifice 300 million Chinese for the victory of the world revolution."[17] Up to 70 million people are believed to have been killed during Mao's reign.[18] Chairman Mao is known to have regarded Darwin and his evolutionist disciple Huxley as his two favourite authors.

1975: Pol Pot

In 1998, the death of Cambodia's Pol Pot marked the end of one of the world's worst mass-murderers. From 1975, he led the Khmer Rouge to commit genocide against his own people in a bloodthirsty regime which was inspired by the communism of Stalin and Mao Zedong. It is estimated that possibly up to 3 million of his own countrymen were killed in his ideological purge (at least one quarter of the population).

© Juandax, Wikimedia Commons

Is history doomed to repeat itself?

And it appears we have short memories and have not learned from history. Leading evolutionary scientists and bioethicists are again calling for controls that echo back to Hitler. Eugenics is the controlled selection of human beings to remove undesirable traits. The 'science' of eugenics was first proposed by Charles Darwin's cousin, Francis Galton. The Nazis took this a step further by conducting surgical experimentation on prisoners in their efforts to produce a superior race. Even in post-war America, eugenics was widespread due to the forced sterilization of 'undesirables'. But after the liberation of Europe when the Nazi death camps were revealed, promoters of eugenics slunk into the shadows.

However, it is making a comeback. Richard Dawkins, for example, has advocated the use of eugenics again today. Rather than the ideas of 'racial hygiene', today's advocates are arguing on the basis of population control or simply of easing the burden and economic expense of looking after those who cannot contribute to the economy of a country, such as the handicapped. Dawkins wrote:

> "[I]f you can breed cattle for milk yield, horses for running speed, and dogs for herding skill, why on Earth should it be impossible to breed humans for mathematical, musical or athletic ability?"

And:

> "I wonder whether, some 60 years after Hitler's death, we might at least venture to ask what the moral difference is between breeding for musical ability and forcing a child to take music lessons. Or why it is acceptable to train fast runners and high jumpers but not to breed them. I can think of some answers, and they are good ones, which would probably end up persuading me."[19]

These seemingly innocuous statements have their roots in a worldview that views mankind as nothing more than animals—the same view as the genocidal despots of the last century. The logical application of such views will inevitably lead to the death of people again. In fact, it is happening today to the most defenseless humans of all by killing unborn children (see later).

A logical or illogical basis for morality?

The mass-murdering communist leaders of the 20th century were inspired by evolutionary ideas. And although it might seem like distant history to some, the philosophy that underpinned their actions is still taught in schools and by the media, although modern evolutionists are quick to distance themselves from practical application of evolutionary principles to humans. But does that mean that there are no evolutionary implications for the value of human life?

As much as we look back in horror at these genocidal regimes, their actions were logically consistent with their belief systems. If mankind just evolved from the primordial ooze along with everything else, there would be no basis for claiming that human life is sacred. So when they gained political power, they used that position to fulfill those ideas. Now someone reading this who also believes in evolution might think the connection is too farfetched, but what if you were one of the ones consigned to Hitler's gas chambers or Stalin's gulags? What logical reasoning could you offer to say that they were wrong in acting on what you both believe to be true?

Nature exhibits all sorts of atrocities in the animal kingdom. Killer whales just eat the lips (the juiciest parts) off fellow whale species and leave them to die. Female spiders and praying mantises eat their mates. Male polar bears and tigers will often hunt down their offspring to eat them, and male lions will kill the offspring of a deposed lion. This causes the mothers to go into heat again so that they can mate with the lionesses. If man looks to the natural world for his inspiration, he will find all sorts of justification to do wrong to other members of his species.

However, if we look to the Bible's explanation of the world's origin, we will see that it was not meant to be this way. The fact that most of us are horrified at the actions of other sinful people, or the brutality of the animal world, should actually cause us to realize that something is wrong.

Now let's be clear. We are not saying a non-Christian or an atheist cannot be moral. But in a materialistic worldview, there is no logical basis for objective morality. History has shown that when mankind tries to define morality apart from God's Word, it can result in the

Genghis Khan

death of millions of people. One can be an atheist and do good things, like charity and community service. But what logical basis— that is, what philosophical reasoning— compels that person to do so? Because it denies the existence of the Creator God, atheism cannot provide any objective basis for the concepts of morality that underpin Western civilization. It's the exact opposite. If nature shows us the way and evolution is the ruling paradigm, then the strong should be allowed to prevail over the weak; after all, 'it's the law of nature'. Why feed starving children in Africa if the local agronomy cannot support the population? These views are the logical extension of beliefs in evolution. If we take this approach, the greatly feared despot Genghis Khan, who raped, pillaged, and murdered his way across Asia and parts of Europe in the 13th century, would be regarded as the greatest evolutionary success story in human history. Researchers have even claimed that up to 8% of Asia's nearly 4 billion people are descended from this Mongol warlord's tribes.[20]

The most commonly understood concepts of morality have a Judeo-Christian basis, because its tenets are founded in the principle that God is Creator and man is made in His image. The Creator who became flesh, Jesus Christ, taught extensively about mankind's role in looking after each other. In His famous discourse in Matthew 5, known as the Sermon on the Mount, He said (among other things):

> "Blessed are the meek, for they shall inherit the earth. … Blessed are the merciful, for they shall receive mercy. … Blessed are the peacemakers, for they shall be called sons of God" (vv. 5, 7, 9).

We all remember the old adages that say 'do unto others', 'love your neighbour as yourself', and the Christian admonitions of feeding the hungry and clothing the poor, and so on. These biblical concepts seek to honour and respect mankind because we are made in His image, and part of that is intuitively or inwardly knowing that it is wrong to murder and steal.

In the image of God

The Bible depicts the creation of man as unique from that of the other land animals:

> "Then God said, 'Let us make man in our image, after our likeness. And let them have dominion over the fish of the sea and over the birds of the heavens and over the livestock and over all the earth and over every creeping thing that creeps on the earth.' So God created man in his own image, in the image of God he created him; male and female he created them" (Genesis 1:26–27).

Mankind was supernaturally created by God from the dust of the ground. Genesis 2:7 then says:

> "then the LORD God formed the man of dust from the ground and breathed into his nostrils the breath of life, and the man became a living creature."

Clearly the Bible is not referring to man's evolution from a lower hominid-type creature. Furthermore, it shows mankind's pre-eminence in the Creator's plan for this world. Our soul is eternal, unlike other creatures, as humans are the only ones who are offered salvation through the blood of their kinsman-redeemer, Christ (Isaiah 59:20). In the New Testament, when tracing Jesus' ancestry back to Adam, Luke called Adam "the son of God" (Luke 3:38) because he was a direct creation of God—in other words, Adam was not the son of Ug the caveman. In Genesis 5, when describing the birth of one of Adam's sons, Seth, it says:

"This is the book of the generations of Adam. When God created man, he made him in the likeness of God. Male and female he created them, and he blessed them and named them Man when they were created. When Adam had lived 130 years, he fathered a son in his own likeness, after his image, and named him Seth" (vv. 1–3).

In Genesis 1, when God created the plants and animals, the phrases "after their kind" or "after his kind" are used 10 times. Note that it says Adam was made in God's likeness but Adam's son was after his own likeness. People often miss this contrast, and it is important because it now reflects our potential to do wrong things and leave God out of the picture.

When the Bible says that humans are made in God's image, it clearly does not mean that we share in all God's attributes, because we are not all-powerful, all-knowing, or present everywhere. Simply, the image of God means that in some ways we resemble God, and we represent Him as His stewards of the physical creation.

Theology professor Wayne Grudem writes:

"When God says, 'Let us make man in our image, after our likeness' (Gen 1:26), the meaning is that God plans to make a creature similar to himself. Both the Hebrew word for 'image' (*tselem*) and the Hebrew word for 'likeness' (*demût*) refer to something that is *similar* but not identical to the thing it represents or is an 'image' of. The word *image* can also be used of something that *represents* something else."[21]

A mental likeness

Man has an intellectual ability that far surpasses any other creature. Such capacity gives us the ability to communicate, not only with one another but also with God Himself. Thus, we should be able to use this ability to understand when God speaks to us (through the Bible) and also to recognize that there is a Creator (Romans 1:20). This mental ability enables us to compose and appreciate music, to reason and do complex mathematics, to laugh and do many things that are distinct from the animal kingdom.

A moral likeness

As mentioned earlier, all humans have an inbuilt moral compass that instinctively tells us right from wrong. When Adam and Eve sinned by disobeying their Creator's instructions for them, they instinctively knew something was wrong. After eating fruit from the tree of the knowledge of good and evil, the Bible says:

> "Then the eyes of both were opened, and they knew that they were naked. And they sewed fig leaves together and made themselves loincloths" (Gen. 3:7).

This indicates that they immediately became self-aware of what they had done. Previously, they were innocent beings before God and being naked was not a problem. It only became a problem after Adam sinned—they were no longer righteous and their sin demanded a covering. The Apostle Paul says that even those who do not have Scripture have God's Law written on their hearts, and that humans have a conscience that will defend or prosecute them based on their deeds. So unlike animals, our actions can be morally good, as when we help others, or evil, such as when we sin.

A social likeness

God's nature is love (1 John 4:8), and He is a social being as displayed in the Trinity (where one God exists as three persons in perfect fellowship with each other). And God created people to have a relationship with Him and each other. Before their Fall, Genesis 3:8 indicates that Adam and Eve walked in the garden with God. While the Fall damaged our relationship with God and each other, we are still relational beings.

A spiritual likeness

We are not solely physical beings, thus we have immaterial spirits, unlike animals. Because of this, we can relate to God and we are held responsible for the revelation we receive both from nature and Scripture about God. Our spiritual nature also means we are eternal; i.e. once we are born, we never cease to exist. When we die, believers will go to Paradise to await the resurrection of our bodies at Christ's (the Creator's) Second Coming.

Where does our spirit come from?

There are two views as to how a person gets his or her spirit. One is called *traducianism* and the other is called *creationism*. *Traducianism* is a view that both the material and immaterial aspect of humans (the soul) are derived from the parents. Thus our sin nature can also be transmitted via this means. This means it would also apply to artificially generated persons from IVF, cloning, and other reproductive technologies. Scriptures used to support this view include Psalm 51:5, John 1:14; 3:6, Romans 5:12, and Hebrews 7:10, as well as the fact that Adam's son Seth was "in his own likeness, after his image" (Genesis 5:3).

The *creationist* view maintains that at conception God creates a new soul for every individual, because God distinguishes the origin of the soul from the origin of the body. This view would cite Scriptures such as Ecclesiastes 12:7; Isaiah 42:5; Zechariah 12:1; and Hebrews 12:9.

While we believe that there is room for both views, we think the one with the most scriptural basis is the traducian view. The creationist view would have God continually creating new human souls, while Genesis indicates that God ceased or rested from creating on Day 7. Additionally, the traducian view better explains how new human souls are infected with sin (because the sin nature is somehow passed on by the parents).

Whichever is correct, both views affirm the biblical view that man is unique and was created in God's image.

Broken images

Before the Fall, humans perfectly reflected the image of God as He intended. Sin distorted but did not destroy that image. Adam passed this distorted image to his children (Genesis 5:3) and down to us today. And because Adam was God's appointed steward of creation, when he sinned, the rest of creation fell, too.

"For we know that the whole creation has been groaning together in the pains of childbirth until now" (Romans 8:22).

Because the creation was cursed, death has taken a terrible toll on the lives of all living creatures. The Bible is clear that there was no death and suffering before Adam's sin: God pronounced that His finished creation was "very good". In addition, in the NT, Romans 5:12 reminds us that:

"sin came into the world through one man, and death through sin, and so death spread to all men because all sinned."

Now, animals rip and tear each other apart because the world is fallen. If we are honest, very few of us are reconciled with death of any sort, whether it is the death of a loved family member or the family pet. To repeat, it should remind us that something is wrong with our world, and it was not a loving God's original intention for creation.

The Bible is also clear that it is an offence to kill another human being (in the OT it carried a death penalty). Man was given dominion over creation but not each other (Genesis 1:28). We said previously that the overwhelming acceptance of evolution has caused many to reject our true origins and has justified some in killing other humans as if they were animals. So, not only is the creation 'broken', and us along with it as His broken image-bearers, it also causes us to view the world and each other through broken lenses.

WORLDVIEWS

EVOLUTION:
Monkeys to mankind
Millions of years
Survival of the fittest
Death & disease
No life after death

CREATION:
Originally good creation
Mankind in God's image
Death because of sin
Redemption / Restoration
Human life is valuable

The set of glasses we use to look at the world is derived from our worldview.
And our worldviews are primarily derived by our beliefs about where we came from.

Salvation partially restores God's image-bearers

Romans 10:9–10 says:

> "if you confess with your mouth that Jesus is Lord and believe in your heart that God raised him from the dead, you will be saved. For with the heart one believes and is justified, and with the mouth one confesses and is saved."

By believing in the sacrifice of God's Son, the Lord Jesus Christ, our sins can be paid for. Jesus (who is God in the flesh) can do this because He is the Creator, and only a sinless man could take our place, and only God could withstand the judgment against sin. When one accepts Christ's atoning work for us, it causes a spiritual transformation in the believer. This is what it means to be 'born again'.

> "Blessed be the God and Father of our Lord Jesus Christ! According to his great mercy, he has caused us to be born again

to a living hope through the resurrection of Jesus Christ from the dead to an inheritance that is imperishable, undefiled, and unfading, kept in heaven for you" (1 Peter 1:3–4).

But we still only bear a marred image of God—we still die, we still sin, we still fall short of what God intended for us (Romans 3:23). We still have the fallen nature due to our flesh; the ultimate solution to the Fall can be nothing less than a complete re-creation—new sinless bodies. And at the end of time, God will destroy this corrupted creation and restore it anew. And, the believers who were paid for by the blood of the Creator Himself will be there.

This 'born again' transformation causes us to look at the world and its inhabitants differently from how we previously looked at such things.

But if God is the Creator, isn't animal life also special?

It is fair to say that if God is Creator and we are here for a purpose, then the same must apply to the rest of His creation, including animals. Indeed, Isaiah 45:18 says:

> "For thus says the LORD, who created the heavens (he is God!), who formed the earth and made it (he established it; he did not create it empty, he formed it to be inhabited!)".

Clearly, it is inhabited by lots of creatures, but the Bible is clear that only man was made in God's image. Therefore, only man was given dominion over the creation in Genesis 1:27–28:

> "So God created man in his own image, in the image of God he created him; male and female he created them. And God blessed them. And God said to them, 'Be fruitful and multiply and fill the earth and subdue it, and have dominion over the fish of the sea and over the birds of the heavens and over every living thing that moves on the earth.'"

This is important to realize because there is another evolutionary mindset that seeks to elevate animals to the same status as human beings, thereby reducing humans who are made in the image of God to the level of mere animals once again.

Animal rights?

Recently, various projects and spokespersons have sought to elevate the status of apes, in particular gorillas and chimpanzees, by attempting to bestow upon them 'human rights'. One such organization called The Nonhuman Rights Project has issued writs before US courts, saying:

> "These *habeas corpus* writs are a way of going before the court to argue that our chimpanzee plaintiffs are legal persons with the fundamental right to bodily liberty, based on their level of complex cognition, self-awareness and autonomy ... ."[22]

Many of these advocates see no difference between a chimp and human child. The basis for all of this thinking is that such apes are our closest living relatives on the evolutionary ladder, 'after all, we were once like them'. To many people this makes sense, but once again, it depends upon your worldview. After all, anyone can visit any zoo, look at chimpanzees, and see that they have two arms, two legs, and display many physical characteristics that are similar to humans. Such similarities often strike a sympathetic and emotional chord. In addition, most people have heard claims that human and chimp DNA is 98% similar. Animal rights activist Steven Wise has said:

> "The science is making it very clear, that chimpanzees are us—they are very close to us—and they have the autonomy that judges care about."[23]

'Banana Lover #1' by Shawn Allen, http://flickr.com/photos/59743169@ N00/18446148. Licence at http:// creativecommons.org/licenses/by/2.0.

But it is not as straightforward as that. Genetics is highly complex, and the quoted DNA figure is highly misleading because similarities depend on what is being compared. For example, one biologist who is sympathetic to the human/chimp DNA claims wrote:

> "For about 23% of our genome, we share no immediate genetic ancestry with our closest living relative, the chimpanzee."[24]

And with regard to the areas that are being compared, some researchers have stated the comparison figure is as low as 65%.[25] But even a 2% difference in human and chimp DNA is equivalent to 60 million base pairs or letters of information. The human genome contains 3 billion letters of information, which if typed out into 500 page books would constitute a pile over 1,000 high. The 2% difference means you'd be reading a lot of different stories.

Given that God used the same language convention (DNA) to create everything, one would naturally expect similarities between living things that aren't thought to be closely related. Sharks and whales possess similar features, but one is a fish and one is a mammal. Similarities are simply due to common design, not common descent. Given the wide genetic gap between humans and apes, there has not been enough time for the multiplication of alleged mutations over millions of years to bridge the gap—even on an evolutionary scale! Common design (and a common language system) actually points to a common Creator for all. It's reminiscent of the famous passage in Romans 1:20:

> "For his invisible attributes, namely, his eternal power and divine nature, have been clearly perceived, ever since the creation of the world, in the things that have been made. So they are without excuse."

Leading evolutionary spokesman Steve Jones said that we share 50% of our genes with bananas and pointed out:

> "that doesn't make us half bananas, either from the waist up or the waist down."[26]

Should we care for the animals?

Jesus said in Luke 12:6–7:

> "Are not five sparrows sold for two pennies? And not one of them is forgotten before God. Why, even the hairs of your head are all numbered. Fear not; you are of more value than many sparrows."

God affirms that He cares for His creation, and as His appointed heads of it, we should therefore look after it. Proverbs 12:10 says:

> "Whoever is righteous has regard for the life of his beast, but the mercy of the wicked is cruel."

And Christians have been at the forefront of exercising responsible stewardship of creation. For example, the RSPCA was established by evangelical, conservative Christians, including William Wilberforce, who also fought to end slavery in Britain. After all, if the creation belongs to the Creator, then we should be good stewards of it in a way that benefits all its inhabitants. But the Bible is also clear that its other creatures should not take precedence over humans. The creation was made for God's glory, but mankind was given stewardship of that creation, including the animals. When looking after the environment, for example, wisdom is needed in applying this biblical principle. This is different from the rabid environmentalism that unfortunately characterizes so much of the debate, which would even displace and disadvantage human beings supposedly to save the environment.

This type of 'over-the-top' environmentalism that seeks to deify nature and elevate animals to human status (or even above) is actually illogical and inconsistent, even by its own evolution-defining standards. As we've said, if evolution were true and mankind is the top of the evolutionary tree, then the likes of Hitler were acting completely consistently with this worldview. Under such a view, it's somewhat illogical to elevate apes and care for them at the expense of humans. After all, if they are our nearest evolutionary relative, then they are also our nearest evolutionary competition. To be consistent, we should have little regard or concern for our evolutionary 'weaker cousins'. The fact that we out-bred and out-performed them is why we are the top of the evolutionary tree anyway. Romans 1:21–23, 25 warns about the tendency of man to elevate nature:

> "For although they knew God, they did not honor him as God or give thanks to him, but they became futile in their thinking, and their foolish hearts were darkened. Claiming to be wise, they became fools, and exchanged the glory of the immortal God for images resembling mortal man and birds and animals and creeping things. … because they exchanged the truth about God for a lie and worshiped and served the creature rather than the Creator, who is blessed forever! Amen."

Genetic engineering (GE): Creating superhumans?

While it may be *permissible* to engage in GE of plants and animals, tinkering at will with an organism's incredibly complex genetic code can easily have unintended consequences. So while we do not oppose such modification in principle, there is the need for thorough testing before any genetically modified organism is marketed for food or released into the environment.

In some ways, the attempt to modify human beings is a logical extension of the success of the same techniques in plants and animals. However, there is an ethical problem: God created man to have dominion over nature, but this dominion does not extend to fellow human beings. Following Christ's example, it is a permissible and good thing to attempt to 'heal' humans. For example, we often implant pig heart valves into humans to save lives. In the same way, surgeons can transplant organs from other humans to save lives. But this is markedly different from attempting to make designer humans by radically altering the human genome. This has been attempted before.

When he came to power, Soviet dictator Joseph Stalin wanted to increase the might of the Red Army and dreamed up the idea of creating super soldiers and workers by breeding humans with apes. He enlisted the help of top animal-breeding scientist Ilya Ivanov and reputedly said to him:

"I want a new invincible human being, insensitive to pain, resistant and indifferent about the quality of food they eat."[27]

Ivanov was dispatched to West Africa to conduct experiments in impregnating chimpanzees with human sperm by artificial insemination, and in later experiments, he tried to use monkey sperm in humans. All the experiments failed completely. All of these shocking details were released when the Russian government released papers from their archives recently. In studying these documents, a Soviet-born, University of Cambridge expert on Russian History, Alexander Etkind revealed the underlying motivation for such experiments:

"If he crossed an ape and a human and produced viable offspring then that would mean Darwin was right about how closely related we are."[28]

It is now well documented that the experiments had an anti-God motive. That is, showing Darwin was right would strike a blow against Christianity, and of course, as we highlighted earlier, it would justify Stalin's culling of human beings with no accountability to the Creator of humans.

Ivanov was no crank and had already gained a reputation as a successful cross-breeder of hybrid animals. The failure of his human/

ape hybrid experiments actually validated the Bible's Creation account, showing that there are breeding limits. While it is possible to interbreed different types of horse species (zebras, donkeys, shire horses, and so on), the Bible says in Genesis 1 that God created distinct kinds ("after their kind"). Humans and apes are distinctly different kinds, meaning that humans did not evolve from apes but were the pinnacle of God's creative power, and it is the reason that conventions that typically apply to animals do not apply to human beings. It is this foundational principle that underpins all moral and ethical arguments with regard to the value of human life.

Designer humans?

For an evolutionist, it is a logical progression from modifying plants and animals to using these same genetic engineering techniques on humans. Recently, the UK government approved the use of a mitochondrial transfer procedure on human embryos that would result in children with DNA from a father and a mother and mitochondrial DNA from an egg donor—three genetic parents! While this was hailed as a breakthrough that will allow women with mitochondrial diseases to have healthy children, the manipulation of the egg causes extensive damage that puts the resultant baby at risk of a whole suite of developmental abnormalities. This would cause the death of many babies who would not make it to birth and cause others to suffer because they would be diseased. This is totally avoidable, so it should be opposed. In addition, some procedures used to create three-parent embryos involve the destruction of existing embryos, so we would oppose those procedures on the same grounds as we oppose embryonic stem cell research.[29]

Stem cells

Stem cells are regarded by many as the probable cure for paralysis and many other conditions, and there have already been impressive results with some stem cell treatments. But, there is a lot of misinformation in this area.

There are two types of stem cells—adult stem cells are derived from umbilical cord blood or bone marrow, as well as a few other places in the human body. A person's own stem cells can be used, meaning there is no risk of rejection in contrast to donated organs.

However, another type of stem cell is the embryonic stem cell. These are 'undifferentiated', meaning they have not yet become specific eye cells, bone cells, etc. But, in reality, this line of stem cells is both ethically unacceptable and less promising as a cure for disease. To get embryonic stem cells, an embryo—a tiny human being—is killed very early in its development for its cells. These cells can be propagated in a stem cell line indefinitely. But years of research have now shown that these are less stable than adult stem cells and are also not as effective for therapeutic uses due to rejection by the recipient's body.[30]

So, while one type of stem cell is uncontroversial and effective, the other is unstable and ethically problematic. Why would one push for funding for the latter type? Clearly, there is an agenda at work, because if it becomes acceptable to create and destroy embryos for medical research that opens the door for more radical 'therapeutic' procedures—for instance, why not gestate a clone until it is large enough to harvest its organs? After all, what is the moral difference between taking apart an embryo for its cells or taking a clone's organs—in other words, making babies for spare parts! They are just different stages of development of the same human entity.

Human cloning

A clone is an exact genetic duplicate of another creature. Some clones occur naturally—identical twins are actually clones of each other, but it happens naturally in the womb without outside interference.

It is now possible, in principle, to create a human clone, and we would suggest it is only a matter of time before someone actually does this. In the process of cloning, a cell is taken from the parent, and the nucleus is transferred to an egg that has had its nucleus removed. The egg is 'tricked' into thinking it has been fertilized and begins developing as an embryo. Many animals have now been cloned.

A major problem with this process is that it is inefficient—it takes many attempts to create a viable clone—meaning that many clones fail to make it to birth. Also, like the famous 'Dolly the sheep' experiment,[31] those that survive have higher rates of disease and deformity and are 'pre-aged' because the DNA in their cells is older (the telomeres are shorter). Because of this, we believe it is an immoral experimentation to try to create a human clone, because it will result in totally avoidable human death and suffering.

Many people wonder: would human clones have souls? The answer is, of course, yes. Just as identical twins develop from one fertilized egg but are two unique individuals, an artificially

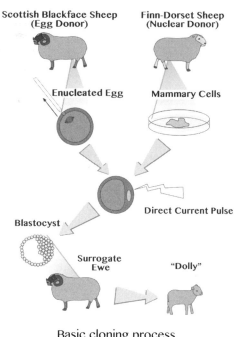

Basic cloning process

produced human clone would have his or her own personality and soul and would be able to be saved through faith in Jesus Christ.[32]

Abortion

In most Western countries, it is legal for a pregnant mother to get an abortion if she does not want the baby. Some countries have extreme abortion laws which allow abortion past the time of viability, even up to the time of birth if it is believed that the mother's emotional well-being or health is at stake. This is despite the testimony of many doctors that there is *no* medical scenario where the abortion of a viable child is necessary to save the life of the mother.

Biologically, it is an indisputable fact that from conception the growing baby is a distinct living organism. The baby will be dependent on the mother's womb to survive and grow throughout the pregnancy, but this does not detract from the fact that the unborn baby is an independent living being.

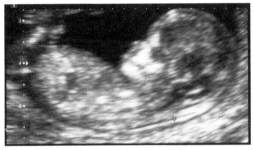

With the development of ultrasound technology, it is impossible to argue that the unborn child is less than fully human—and abortionists know this. One abortionist who kills babies as late as six months along said, "Am I killing? Yes, I am. I know that."[33] We can now see the baby's heartbeat just six weeks after conception. A baby only a few months after conception can be seen kicking and sucking his or her thumb. And horrifyingly, ultrasound also shows that pre-born babies struggle to try to get away from the implements of the abortionist and scream silently as they are dismembered.[34] But so much of this evidence is withheld from the public and many women considering abortions, so they often do not make fully informed decisions. So, many people today still think that abortion is just removing a 'lump of cells' or that the baby is less than fully human.[35]

Because it is impossible in this age to argue that the child is less than human, the debate in recent years has shifted towards 'personhood'. Abortion advocates will say that because the child is undeveloped he or she is not yet a 'person' with rights, or at least any rights the child has cannot overrule a mother who decides she does not want to be pregnant. However, Scripture treats the unborn child as human from conception on (see the Scripture list in the appendix). The word that Scripture uses for the child in the womb is the same as it uses for an infant outside the womb. And Scripture *never* separates the concepts of 'human' and 'person'. So if a baby is a living human being (which he or she demonstrably is from the moment of conception) in the biblical view, he or she is a *person* whom God the Creator commands us not to murder. This argument about personhood is also a very dangerous ground to tread because one could twist such views to apply to children who are a few months to a few years old! And in fact, some people have done this; Peter Singer, the infamous Australian 'ethicist', has advocated for parents to be able to kill their new baby up to 28 days after birth.[36]

What about miscarriage?

Sometimes, tragically, a mother miscarries and her child dies in the womb. The mother is *not* guilty because she did nothing to cause the death of the child. Many times a miscarriage is caused because of something that went wrong in the development of the baby, and such things unfortunately occur in a fallen world.

Some argue that the high rate of miscarriage in pregnancy makes the unborn child less valuable than born children. However, all of us are mortal—some simply die very early in life. Just because humans have a 100% mortality rate does not mean that human life is not valuable! Similarly, the percentage of pregnancies that miscarry does not affect the value of the unborn child.[37]

What if the mother was raped?

Many people who call themselves pro-life allow for an exception in cases of rape and incest. Everyone should be appalled when these crimes happen and call for harsh penalties for people who commit them. We should also ensure that the woman who is the victim of such an attack receives the support she needs.

The child who is conceived in such circumstances is another *victim* of his or her father—not another assailant, and so should not receive the death penalty for the circumstances of his or her conception. The answer to a horrific act of violence against a woman is not to commit another act of violence against her *and* her baby. One woman who later regretted her abortion said, "I got over the rape but I never got over my abortion experience." She tells other women facing the same circumstance, "Think twice. Don't go into having an abortion because it's a quick fix—it's not. That abortion experience will stay with you for the rest of your life. It will haunt you."[38]

Some women decide to keep their babies conceived in rape, and they turn out to be a huge blessing in their family, showing how God can bring good out of the worst circumstances if we decide to properly love an innocent child. In other cases, the mother decides to give up her baby for adoption. This is a loving and praiseworthy action: it gives the baby a chance to grow up with a mother and father who otherwise may never have had a child. Also, a young mother could have a chance to finish school and pursue life goals knowing that she has given her baby a chance at a good life.

What about when the mother's health or life is in danger?

Sometimes, a pregnancy will endanger the health or life of the mother, posing the most troubling question for pro-life people. Sometimes, the complications of a pregnancy can be life-threatening for a woman. When possible, every measure should be taken to preserve the life of *both* mother and baby. But sometimes this is not possible, and the baby must be removed to save the life of the mother. The primary case where this happens today is the case of ectopic pregnancy, where the fertilized egg implants and the baby begins to grow somewhere other than the womb—most often in the fallopian tube. This results in life-threatening complications for the mother, so the baby must be removed. It is really the only option to save one of their lives, because if the mother dies, then there would be no way to keep the baby alive at so early a stage of development.

Note, this is different from abortion where the goal is to kill the baby. In the case of ectopic pregnancies, for example, the goal of the operation is to save the mother's life in a situation where the baby could not survive in any case.

While these 'hard cases' are cited as reasons why abortion needs to be available to women, the *vast majority* of abortions are not because of rape or the health of the mother—they are elective procedures because, for whatever reason (i.e. economic or social), the woman does not want to be pregnant. But abortion advocates raise rape and the life of the mother as reasons for abortion to be legal—then promptly demand abortion in any circumstance at any stage of pregnancy.

What about when the baby is severely disabled?

Sometimes when a disability or disease is detected in the womb, the mother is pressured to abort. For instance, around 90% of women who receive a prenatal diagnosis of Down syndrome will abort their

sons and daughters rather than giving birth to a disabled child. Consistent with his worldview, evolutionist Richard Dawkins even made the statement that abortion is the "moral" choice when a baby is diagnosed with Down syndrome.[39]

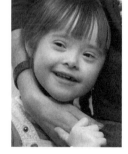

As Christians, we recognize that our value as human beings does not come from being physically or mentally 'perfect' or from what contributions we can make to society. It is wrong to abort a child even if he or she will only live a short time outside the womb. Also, there are many accounts of children diagnosed as 'incompatible with life' (a description that is often used for babies who are expected to die in the womb or shortly after birth because of genetic conditions or developmental abnormalities) who went on to defy the doctors' expectations and live healthy lives.

Sadly, the acceptability of abortion in cases of fetal disability is such that sometimes people go on to sue for 'wrongful birth' if a fetal abnormality was not detected.[40] This leaves doctors vulnerable, so they often advocate abortion on suspicion of an abnormality.

When a child dies soon after birth from a disease, we recognize that it is a result of the Fall and a great tragedy. But when that same child is aborted, the child is not killed by the disease but by the abortionist in an extremely painful and inhumane manner, and it is breaking one of the Creator's commandments, namely, "You shall not murder" (Exodus 20:13).

'Gendercide': When a baby isn't wanted because she is a girl

Most western advocates of abortion believe it is wrong to procure an abortion because a baby is the 'wrong' gender, but this is a growing problem, especially in China, where the one-child policy has resulted in an exaggerated son preference, and in India, where girls are viewed as expensive due to the tradition of giving a dowry when a girl is married. Sex selection is so prevalent in these areas that millions of men are growing up with no chance of finding a bride.

The pro-choice person can hardly condemn a woman who chooses to get an abortion based on her baby's sex. If she can abort because she doesn't want a baby, she must also be able to abort because she doesn't want a baby girl. Only someone with a pro-life view has the *consistent* grounds to condemn these abortions across the board.[41]

The problem: Commoditization of children

Much of the abortion problem stems from a wrong view of children as commodities. In other words, the idea is that "I am owed a perfect baby" if I want one, no matter the collateral damage that may result. For instance, in principle there is no problem with IVF, but in practice, it commoditizes children. Often, many more embryos are created than will be implanted—the 'extras' are kept on ice for up to 10 years before they are discarded. The fate of these children is uncertain—as the 'property' of the parents, these tiny children can be kept on ice indefinitely. And the longer they are kept frozen, the more likely they will not be able to survive and develop if they are transferred to a womb (either that of their biological mother, a surrogate, or an adoptive mother). Also, if an IVF treatment results in a multiple pregnancy, the woman may 'reduce' the pregnancy by aborting the 'extra' child or children.

The problem is that once we commoditize one group of people, other groups of people are soon to follow. For instance, various groups of women are being commoditized as egg donors and surrogates—their eggs and wombs are being viewed as 'products' to be bought for another person's ends. So, we should think carefully before allowing things that advance the commoditization of human beings.

However, when we see each baby as a unique person created in God's image with a soul from his or her very earliest existence, we won't be able to bear the thought of keeping these innocent and precious babies on ice in IVF clinics, or killing them in the womb.

Euthanasia or physician-assisted suicide—is it moral?

When life is attacked at its very beginning, it is only natural for people to depreciate it at other vulnerable stages. There is a growing movement to allow people with terminal illnesses and the elderly to commit suicide by taking lethal amounts of various medications—supervised by a doctor. Some US states and European countries have already legalized physician-assisted suicide.

But what does this say about the value of terminally ill and elderly people who *don't* want to prematurely end their lives? Rather, as a society, we should be caring for these people, not pressuring them to die—because the 'right to die' can very easily become the 'duty to die'. And quickly our notions about what sort of life is or isn't worth living can end up killing people.

All of us must face death. Sometimes this is in horrific circumstances, or much earlier than we would like. And at that time, hospice is an option that allows a person to be comfortably medicated and make the most of precious time with loved ones, while not taking one's death into his or her own hands.[42]

The real problem: Sin

We are living with the consequences of Adam's rebellion—but many argue that it is unfair for us to be punished for what Adam did. However, the sinful nature we inherit means that we willfully rebel against God; we deserve His condemnation because we are sinful in both our nature and our actions, but:

"God shows his love for us in that while we were still sinners, Christ died for us" (Romans 5:8).

Salvation partially restores God's image bearers

Romans 10:9–10 says:

"if you confess with your mouth that Jesus is Lord and believe in your heart that God raised him from the dead, you will be saved. For with the heart one believes and is justified, and with the mouth one confesses and is saved."

By believing in the sacrifice of God's Son, the Lord Jesus Christ, our sins can be paid for. Jesus (who is God in the flesh) can do this because He is the Creator, and only a sinless man could take our place, and only God could withstand the judgment against sin. When one accepts Christ's atoning work for us, it causes a spiritual transformation in the believer. This is what it means to be 'born again'.

"Blessed be the God and Father of our Lord Jesus Christ! According to his great mercy, he has caused us to be born again to a living hope through the resurrection of Jesus Christ from the dead to an inheritance that is imperishable, undefiled, and unfading, kept in heaven for you" (1 Peter 1:3–4).

But we still only bear a marred image of God—we still die, we still sin, we still fall short of what God intended for us (Romans 3:23). We still have the fallen nature due to our flesh; the ultimate solution to the Fall can be nothing less than a complete re-creation—new sinless bodies. And at the end of time God will destroy this corrupted Creation and restore it anew. And the believers who were paid for by the blood of the Creator Himself will be there.

This 'born again' transformation causes us to look at the world and its inhabitants differently from how we previously looked at such things.

Life in the light of eternity

Anything we can do to extend life is temporary, because we will all face death. But destroying life is also temporary, because death is not the end of human existence. Scripture tells us, "it is appointed for man to die once, and after that comes judgment" (Hebrews 9:27). We will spend forever either in the presence of God, or away from Him in a place of judgment. All of us deserve to be judged and go to Hell because we've all sinned against God. But God loves us so much that

He provided a way to be forgiven and to spend eternity with Him.

Jesus, God the Son, became a man and lived a perfectly sinless life. Then He died in our place, taking the penalty for sin so that anyone who believes in Him can be forgiven. This allows us to be admitted to Heaven when we die. And Jesus promises that those who believe in Him will be resurrected in perfect bodies, and we will live in a new world with no death or suffering of any kind—the way God originally created it.

APPENDIX: SCRIPTURE INDEX

The use of the 'image of God' in the Bible

Genesis 1:26–27: "Then God said, 'Let us make man in our image, after our likeness. And let them have dominion over the fish of the sea and over the birds of the heavens and over the livestock and over all the earth and over every creeping thing that creeps on the earth.' So God created man in his own image, in the image of God he created him; male and female he created them."

Genesis 5:1b: "When God created man, he made him in the likeness of God."

Genesis 9:6: "Whoever sheds the blood of man, by man shall his blood be shed, for God made man in his own image."

Romans 8:29: "For those whom he foreknew he also predestined to be conformed to the image of his Son, in order that he might be the firstborn among many brothers."

James 3:9–10: "With it [the tongue] we bless our Lord and Father, and with it we curse people who are made in the likeness of God. From the same mouth come blessing and cursing. My brothers, these things ought not to be so."

Scriptures indicating the value of human life

Exodus 21:12: "Whoever strikes a man so that he dies shall be put to death."

Psalm 8:4–5: "What is man that you are mindful of him, and the son of man that you care for him? Yet you have made him a little lower than the heavenly beings and crowned him with glory and honor."

Matthew 6:26: "Look at the birds of the air: they neither sow nor reap nor gather into barns, and yet your heavenly Father feeds them. Are you not of more value than they?"

Scriptures indicating humanity of the unborn

Genesis 25:22–23: "The children struggled together within her, and she said, 'If it is thus, why is this happening to me?' So she went to inquire of the LORD. And the Lord said to her, 'Two nations are in your womb, and two peoples from within you shall be divided; the one shall be stronger than the other, the older shall serve the younger.'"

Exodus 21:22–25: "When men strive together and hit a pregnant woman, so that her children come out, but there is no harm, the one who hit her shall surely be fined, as the woman's husband shall impose on him, and he shall pay as the judges determine. But if there is harm, then you shall pay life for life, eye for eye, tooth for tooth, hand for hand, foot for foot, burn for burn, wound for wound, stripe for stripe."

Judges 13:5: "For behold, you shall conceive and bear a son. No razor shall come upon his head, for the child shall be a Nazirite to God from the womb, and he shall begin to save Israel from the hand of the Philistines."

Psalm 22:9–10: "Yet you are he who took me from the womb; you made me trust you at my mother's breasts. On you was I cast from my birth, and from my mother's womb you have been my God."

Psalm 139:13–16: "For you formed my inward parts; you knitted me together in my mother's womb. I praise you, for I am fearfully and wonderfully made. Wonderful are your works; my soul knows it very well. My frame was not hidden from you, when I was being made in secret, intricately woven in the depths of the earth. Your eyes saw my unformed substance; in your book were written, every one of them, the days that were formed for me, when as yet there was none of them."

Jeremiah 1:5: "Before I formed you in the womb I knew you, and before you were born I consecrated you; I appointed you a prophet to the nations."

Endnotes

1. Defined as the part of the world that had a long heritage of being based on Christian principles.

2. Dawkins, R., *The Blind Watchmaker*, Penguin, London, p. 6, 1991.

3. Wilson, E.O., *From so Simply a Beginning*, Norton, New York, p. 12, 2006.

4. Hitler, A., *Mein Kampf,* greatwar.nl/books/meinkampf/meinkampf.txt, accessed 30 March 2015.

5. Such as *Victims of the Past* (*Opfer der Vergangenheit*), 1937.

6. See creation.com/the-darwinian-roots-of-the-nazi-tree-weikart-review. Note: Hitler was scientifically wrong with these claims. Natural selection is not the same as evolution because selection can only work on what is already present in a population. It cannot create any new features that particles-to-people evolution requires. See creation.com/natural-selection-questions-and-answers.

7. Euthanasia and newborn infants, government.nl/issues/euthanasia/euthanasia-and-newborn-infants, 14 June 2015.

8. Smith-Spark, L. and Magnay, D., Belgium: Lawmakers vote for children's 'right to die' euthanasia law, *CNN*, 13 February 2014, cnn.com.

9. Smith, W., Involuntary euthanasia rampant in Belgium, 10-year review says, *LifeNews.com*, 12 December 2012, Lifenews.com.

10. Grigg, R. and Sarfati, J., Genocide, evolution and the Bible, 5 October 2007, creation.com/genocide-evolution-and-the-bible.

11. Adapted from creation.com/charles-darwins-impact-the-bloodstained-legacy-of-evolution.

12. *The Religion of Social Darwinism,* gennet.org/index.php?option=com_content&view=article&id=65:, 19 June 2015.

13. Jacoby, J., To the victims of Communism: lest we forget, *The Boston Globe*, 7 December 1995, jeffjacoby.com/5935/to-the-victims-of-communism-lest-we-forget.

14. Eastman, M., *Trotsky: A portrait of his youth*, New York, pp. 117–118, 1925; quoted in Woolley, B., The Darwin/Trotsky connection, *Creation* **23**(2):54–55, 2001, creation.com/darwin-trotsky-connection.

15. Communist Democide, hawaii.edu/powerkills/COM.TAB1.GIF, 19 June 2015.

16. This Century's Bloodiest Dictators, hawaii.edu/powerkills/DBG.TAB1.4.GIF, 19 June 2015.

17. Chang, J. and Halliday, J., *Mao: The Unknown Story* (Jonathan Cape, 2005), pp. 411, 457–458; quoted in Ammi, K., Atheism, 11 June, 2009, creation.com/atheism.

18. Mao Zedong, *Wikipedia*, wikipedia.org/wiki/Mao_Zedong, 2 June 2015.

19. Dawkins, R., *Scotland's Sunday Herald*; quoted in White, H., Anti-religion extremist Dawkins advocates eugenics, *Life Site*, 21 November 2006, lifesite-news.com/news/anti-religion-extremist-dawkins-advocates-eugenics.

20. Are you descended from Genghis Khan?, *Examiner*, 11 June 2011, examiner.com/article/are-you-descended-from-genghis-khan.

21. Grudem, W., *Systematic Theology*, Zondervan, Grand Rapids, Michigan, p. 442, 1994.

22. New York Cases – Judges' Decisions and Next Steps, nonhumanrightsproject.org, 10 December 2013; quoted in Nunn, W., Activist challenges judges to redefine chimpanzees' legal status, 15 April 2014, creation.com/chimpanzees-legal-rights.

23. The Nonhuman Rights Project: The Struggle for Legal Personhood for Nonhuman Animals, ieet.org, 16 December 2013; quoted in Nunn, ref. 19.

24. Ebersberger, I. *et al.*, Mapping human genetic ancestry, *Molec. Biol. Evol.* **24**:2266–2276, 2007; quoted in Tomkins, J. and Bergman, J., Genomic monkey business—estimates of nearly identical human-chimp DNA similarity re-evaluated using omitted data, *J. Creation* **26**(1):94–100, 2012, creation.com/chimp.

25. Extracted from a table in Tomkins *et al.*, ref. 21, creation.com/chimp.

26. Jones, S., interviewed at the Australian Museum on The Science Show, broadcast on ABC radio, 12 January 2002, abc.net.au/radionational/programs/scienceshow/almost-like-a-whale/3504048, 13 February 2012; quoted in Doyle, S., Making a man out of a chimp, 1 June 2007, creation.com/making-a-man-out-of-a-chimp.

27. Stephen, C. and Hall, A., Stalin's half-man, half-ape super warriors, *The Scotsman*, 2 August 2006, news.scotsman.com/international.cfm?id=2434192005; quoted in Grigg, R., Stalin's ape-man Superwarriors, *Creation* **29**(1):32–33, 2006, creation.com/stalins-ape-man-superwarriors.

28. Etkind, A., Beyond eugenics: the forgotten scandal of hybridizing humans and apes, *Studies in History and Philosophy of Biological and Biomedical Sciences* **39**(2):205–210, 2008; quoted in Catchpoole, D., Ivanov's ape-human hybrid project—Why?, 11 November 2008, creation.com/ivanovs-ape-human-hybrid-project-why.

29. Three-parent embryos: What should biblical creationists think?, 7 March 2015, creation.com/three-parent-embryos.

30. For more information, see Sarfati J., Stem cells and Genesis, 2001, creation.com/stem-cells.

31. For more information, see More Clone Deaths, *Creation* **26**(1)7–9, 2003, creation.com/focus-261, 5 March 2015.

32. For more information, see creation.com/human-cloning-science-vs-morality.

33. Graas, L., Late-term abortion practitioner: "Yes I am killing" babies, *LifeNews. com*, 14 November 2011, lifenews.com/2011/11/14/late-term-abortion-practitioner-yes-i-am-killing-babies.

34. Cosner, L., When does the unborn baby feel pain?, 22 July 2010, creation.com/unborn-baby-fetal-pain-abortion.

35. An idea popularized by flawed illustrations like Haeckel's embryos— see creation.com/rehabilitating-haeckel.

36. Singer, P. *Rethinking Life and Death: The Collapse of Our Traditional Ethics*, Prometheus Books, New York, p. 130, 217, 1995; quoted in Flynn, D., *Intellectual Morons: How Ideology Makes Smart People Fall for Stupid Ideas*, Crown Forum, New York, p. 74, 2004.

37. Abortions vs miscarriages, creation.com/abortions-vs-miscarriages, 17 March 2013.

38. Ertelt, S., Woman who had an abortion at 13 after rape: "I got over the rape, I'll never get over the abortion", *LifeNews.com*, 14 November 2014, lifenews. com/2014/11/14/woman-who-had-abortion-at-13-after-rape-i-got-over-the-rape-ill-never-get-over-the-abortion/.

39. Cosner, L., Richard Dawkins: Dolphins worth more than babies with Down Syndrome?, 24 August 2014, creation.com/dawkins-ds-abortion.

40. Cosner, L., A 'wrongful birth'?, 16 November 2007, creation.com/a-wrongful-birth.

41. Cosner, L., Abortion: an indispensable right or violence against women?, 6 February 2007, creation.com/abortsex.

42. Cosner, L., Can we choose our end?, 8 November 2014, creation.com/assisted-suicide.

RECOMMENDED RESOURCES

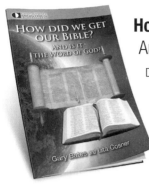

How Did We Get Our Bible?
And is it the Word of God?

Demonstrates historically and practically how the books we have today came to be the Bible—the biggest-selling and most-read book in human history. Christians will be encouraged in their faith by having adequate answers to defend their belief in the authority of Scripture. This booklet is ideal for those new in the faith and will also be suitable as a witnessing resource to non-believers.

Gay Marriage: Right or Wrong?
And who decides?

Openly and frankly discusses the facts and helps clear away much of the confusion and misinformation that characterizes this debate. Both scientifically and biblically sound, it displays genuine compassion while at the same time not shirking the truth. This is a must-read for anyone intending to engage this issue.

Evolution's Achilles' Heels

Exposes the fatal flaws of evolutionary thinking. Like no other work, it is authored by nine Ph.D. scientists to produce a coherent, powerful argument. *Evolution's Achilles' Heels* directly demolishes the very pillars of the belief system that underpins our now-secular culture—evolutionary naturalism. It is coupled with the biblical command to reach the lost with the Good News. In a nutshell, it is a comprehensive outreach tool like no other.

AVAILABLE AT:

CREATION.com

CREATION.com

For more information on creation/evolution and Bible-science issues

---

AUSTRALIA
Creation Ministries International (Australia)
PO Box 4545
Eight Mile Plains, Qld 4113

Phone: (07) 3340 9888
Fax: (07) 3340 9889

CANADA
Creation Ministries International (Canada)
300 Mill St,
Unit 7, Kitchener, ON N2M 5G8

Phone: (519) 746–7616
Orders & donations: 1-888-251-5360
Fax: (519) 746–7617

NEW ZEALAND
Creation Ministries International (NZ)
PO Box 39005
Howick, Auckland 2145

Phone/Fax: (09) 537 4818

SINGAPORE
Creation Ministries International (Singapore)
Clementi Central Post Office
PO Box 195
Singapore 911207

Phone: 9698 4292

SOUTH AFRICA
Creation Ministries International (SA)
PO Box 3349
Durbanville 7551

Phone: (021) 979 0107
Fax: (086) 519 0555

UK & Europe
Creation Ministries International
(UK/Europe)
15 Station St,
Whetstone, Leicestershire, LE8 6JS

Phone: 0116-2848-999

USA
Creation Ministries International (USA)
PO Box 350
Powder Springs, GA 30127

Phone: 800-616-1264
Fax: (770) 439 9784

OTHER COUNTRIES
Creation Ministries International
PO Box 4545
Eight Mile Plains, Qld 4113
Australia

Phone: +617 3340 9888
Fax: +617 3340 9889